T0083843

ABOUT NIGHT

OTHER POETRY BOOKS BY
DENNIS SCHMITZ

We Weep for Our Strangeness
(Big Table Books, Follett Publishing Co., 1969)

Goodwill, Inc.
(Ecco Press, 1975)

String
(Ecco Press, 1980)

Singing
(Ecco Press, 1985)

Eden
(University of Illinois Press, 1989)

ABOUT NIGHT

SELECTED AND NEW POEMS

Dennis Schmitz

FIELD POETRY SERIES
OBERLIN COLLEGE PRESS

ACKNOWLEDGMENTS

THE POEMS IN "NEW POEMS" PREVIOUSLY APPEARED IN:

American Poetry Review: About Night, Chicago Plastics, 1960

FIELD: Birds, Eeyore, Anna Karenina, Rafting, Italy: Carrara #8,
The Ladder: Roger Vail's Photo of a Rockface in the
Carrara (Italy) Marble Quarries, Roger Vail's Photo
of a Worked-Out Mountain in the Carrara (Italy)
Marble Quarries

The Journal: Willensstark

Zyzzyva: Ball

First published by Oberlin College Press in 1993
Rice Hall, Oberlin College
Oberlin, Ohio 44074

Library of Congress Cataloging in Publication Data
Schmitz, Dennis, 1937 / *About Night*

(*FIELD* Poetry Series; 1) / I. Title.
L.C. # 93-083761
ISBN 0-932440-62-2 / ISBN 0-932440-61-4 pbk.

Dennis Schmitz would like to thank the National Endowment
for the Arts and California State University, Sacremento
University Research Committee and Oberlin College Press
would like to thank the Ohio Arts Council, William Goldman,
Lucy & Ralph Hirschmann, and Laurence Perrine for generous
support toward funding this book.

FOR LORETTA

CONTENTS

I FROM *We Weep for Our Strangeness* (1969)

Eclogues /1
If I Could Meet God /4
Virgil: Georgics, Book IV /5

II FROM *Goodwill, Inc.* (1975)

Chicago: Near West-Side Renewal /9
Goodwill, Inc. /12
Queen of Heaven Mausoleum /14
The California Phrasebook /15
Poke-Pole Fishing /18
Tattoo Artist /19

III FROM *String* (1980)

Delta Farm /23
Divining /27
Infinities /28
Rabbits /29
Mile Hill /30
A Rabbit's Death /31
The Man Who Buys Hides /32
String /36
Dog /37
Soup /38
Arbeit Macht Frei /39
In Bosch's World /41
Wings /43
Planting Trout in the Chicago River /44
Making Chicago /46

IV F R O M *Singing* (1985)

Singing /51
A Picture of Okinawa /53
Kindergarten /54
Stung /56
Dressing Game /57
Cutting Out a Dress /58
A Letter to Ron Silliman on the
    Back of a Map of the Solar System /59
Sabotage /61
News /65
The Coal Bin Imagined from My
    Grandmother's Description /67
Gill Boy /69
Attic /70
Lucky Tiger /72
1942 /74

V F R O M *Eden* (1989)

Instructions for Fishing the Eel /79
Bird-Watching /81
Harness /83
Good Friday /85
Driving with One Light /87
Halloween /89
The Pour /91
Climbing Sears Tower /93
Sterno /95
Zoo /96
Halloween-Creature /98
The Grand Egress /100

Instructions for Rowing /102
Matthew's Lesson /104
Catfishing /105
Blue /107
The Spider /109
Ladder /110
La Traviata /112
So High /114
Eden /116

VI   *New Poems*

About Night /121
Willensstark /123
Birds /125
Eeyore /127
Anna Karenina /129
Ball /131
Rafting /133
Italy: Carrara #8 /135
The Ladder: Roger Vail's Photo of a Rockface
      in the Carrara (Italy) Marble Quarries /137
Roger Vail's Photo of a Worked-Out Mountain
      in the Carrara (Italy) Marble Quarries /139
Chicago Plastics, 1960 /141

I

FROM

We Weep for Our Strangeness

1969

ECLOGUES

Where I lived the river
      lay like a blue wrist
between the bluffs & the islands
were tiny unctions of green. Where
      every morning the horses outside
my house woke the sun & their breath
was like wet foliage
      in the cool air. But in my house
my bedroom poised
      between shadow & light & the light
was flawed by angles of glass
till night disappeared in a moment
      of wonder. The farm fed
on the full hillsides & sheets
of grain seemed to fall
      almost to the river's shore.
But from my window the farm
      was less real: the river & at noon
the fish I could almost hear fading
in its cool depths distracted
      the boy of twelve. My brother
beside me
      slept. He was oldest & duty
has deliberate solitude: even my sisters
kept their dolls
      quietly.

The second son: his father
is silent. Whose hands are fouled
      with the birth of a new foal & the brother
fixes the blanket
over the mare's belly. The blood! & the younger
      boy thinks the flesh
a burden & at fault
      for its own pain. The others

lift the foal & pull
the small genital till it flexes
with full life.
    I stood in the barn
born second of God's beasts
    & alone in the days of my making.

My grandfather's God
guided him to the river & the Holy
    Ghost, he said, hung
like a white hand over this hill. Our farm
    was his & when he died
my father (his son) worked a stone
in the shape of a bird, wings
    upraised as if startled
by my grandfather's death.

My name came from the river
the Fox called "Father" &
    "Source" as if a man's semen
were the only cause & my mother's fluid
    a mere aspiration. My mother
told of monsters who may
have died in the river-bed & she read
    that ice a mile high once
moved over their bones. At night
    the river with cold friction
pushes my slumbering flesh
    & my manhood moves
new
& in its own seed.

My father
    died, feeder of so many horses & so fine
an ear he had

he heard the birds with feathered weight
        drop between the green rows
of corn. A gothic
man knowing no
wisdom & in that field we
        no longer plant. The birds
forever float
        above his grave & the ground
gives
more each year.

That winter the farm
        dozed, its tillage deep
in snow. The river
backs a cruel spine against
        the bluffs & boyhood's
dim fish ride
up under the ice, Mother:
        your children. Inside
the fire rubs
itself for warmth & the windows
go white with frost.

if I could meet God
as an animal
my mouth filled with grass
I would not talk
for he knows the smell
of grass
& the great choking
one must have
who seeks to swallow
his world
when an animal dies
his choking is not laughter
he does not shuffle
like a man who forgets
his key
he knows there is no door
he walks inside himself
his belly full
his ears erect with certainty

the wonder
of the bees who
do not mate
for love nor bear
children
in birth-throes
they take their kind
from flowers
in their mouths
they take
their young
the king is kept
in ritual
for ritual they fashion
halls of wax
often
in wandering their wings
are crushed
against a rock
& the heavy body
dies
such is their love
of flowers
& their pride
in honey-making

II

FROM

Goodwill, Inc.

1 9 7 5

CHICAGO: NEAR WEST-SIDE RENEWAL

Sleep was only a dream
Death had of us—
I am afraid to touch
the wall that might be
too warm,
the house that bore its gifts
through the night
till the wet sun lapped at the windows.

What is the good news I should send
of the sealed landscapes, corners
remembered by light—
yesterday's body has traveled
over the same bones to the older
man who crawls,

his young belly bare against the rug.
He raises a hand suddenly dipped
in the sun's fresh golden
spoor who tried to wake only
in the empty lots, to recover his own
spoor before he woke.

Too late! The roads lick up
every kind of weather. Inside, my breath
returned, a tired rider,
hunter, wet with the sweat of his beast.
Before the keyhole's half-
lit eye, the humid dreams drift— like
flawed glass showing the night

we dimly saw, the common death that
stirred under the small crown
of the gas-ring, the domestic sadness
in the wallpaper's distant

foliage. At night a man discards
the daytime face, the flat
map of his globular, primitive heart—
he is home & loneliness is the local
weather.

All night long we built this house,
body by body,
because after the flesh spreads
its natural foliage,
after our roots will pull
up only pain & we refer
to ourselves in the plural,
your bitterness becomes my bitterness,

& it is not enough to nail
a wife in Sunday
love, or if you are a woman, drive
your teeth again & again
into the walls of widowhood.
Instead you are a day-laborer
the Housing Authority hires,
rural white, Southern black, planting

enormous blisters in the palms
you press to the old
walls papered with flowers rippling
under the wrecking ball's rusty sun.
The bricks, worm-riddled joists,
spineless linoleum & lintels
by which the dead left
unused lengths of body preserved

in a permanent coat of fever:
this is our neighborhood broken
breath by breath
from our fathers. Forty feet above
the broached foundation
only plumbing holds the bathroom
walls painted with the names
of the wrong loves, initials in the hearts—
the graffiti a visitor,
the lover who was a guest, leaves.

GOODWILL, INC.

Caught at hanger's ends, the limp
trousers suspended
from zippers like fish surprised
at what they carried:
a king's ring or the genitals
that float like the air bladders
behind the fish's gills & take life
from the liquid where an alien heavy-

bodied animal may drown.
The belts, brassieres & galluses
with their elastic gone
in the orbits the bodies pulled
apart as they circled

each other. The big woman's
girdle broken
by buttocks that moved
like moons around her sex
till she strips
at night to that dark,
reflected light a husband

sheds as he travels
in her stunning gravity.
Love, against your bin of odd
sizes I leaned last—
broken shoes, the borrowed old
man's digestion of a dead
wife who still travels the seamless
loneliness of his insides, or
that first love like a rare food
which went to fat about his loins.

In the dirty changing-room men &
women must share, I assume other
men's clothes, as many as I can put
on of ever-larger sizes
till I stumble & weave

other, richer lives on my own.

QUEEN OF HEAVEN MAUSOLEUM

White as coal-ash pressed
again in veins, fuel for the living
I lay all summer in the fourth

floor crypts chipping
the excess we poured in the footings
for the dead. The foreman kneels

to hand in the tools,
his face framed by this inner
world square as an oven
in which my flesh warmed
death's inspired
ingredients. Which was my hand
& which the dead hand wanting to pry
open the future, the concrete

forms a dead father reinforces
as he fills his son's
teetering flesh. After a moment
my eyes film, magnify
sparks dropping from the darkness
like snowflakes. I fall
back into the frozen position

of the dead or the foetus I once saw
in the clear, icy jacket of a jar.
Around my ankles something tightens
& pulls my legs straight—
in this second, more awkward birth,
when the grinning foreman slaps
me from my faint, will I cry

to be buried, or gratefully begin
to nurse at the world I thirsted for?

West of the Sierras where
the Central Valley
drifts on its crusts of almond
orchards, the fields
die in a holiday accident,
the freeways snapping
back in the dust like severed
arteries while the accomplished
doctor of silence stitches the evening
closed with stoplights which
never hold. Gardens go
on their knees to the sun,
all summer turning
over the brief counterfeit the rain
leaves, looking for a real
coin. In the arbors, the Italian
uncles sit stirring anise-flavored
coffees, red bandanas
over their knees pulsing
with the sweating
body's rhythm like an open
chest in which the transplanted
organ of the homeland has not yet
begun to function.

In East Bay, beyond the Valley
towns, pore to pore
the children, black & brown,
press out a test pattern
of veins, their faces rigid with long
division. They stand
in front of the blackboards looking
for their features, refusing
to draw the white mark
of a dollarsign while the mayor

waits & all the examining
board of cops waits, correction
texts trembling in their hands.
Why must we repeat our lessons—
let us go. In the alleys we rehearse
the lonely patrol of hands
over each other's bodies.
If we unfold a woman's creases,
we are afraid to read
the platitudes. The black
penis is the last piece
of the puzzle we put in place
before the streetlamps have slipped
away in the wet fingers of the April
night, before the pathways
through the asphalt gardens
disgorge the feathers of the black
angel.

You who arrived late
from some forgotten Kansas
laminated of wheat & the sweet
alfalfa wasted with incurable winter
take root in the familiar
flat Valley where the only
winter is overweight with rain,
again & again welling up in fallen,
wet fruit an early unearned
bitterness— like the bum who drowses
under the indelible azaleas scrawled
against the capitol's white
walls. His life too
is a fragrant perennial.
He is less foreign than you,
but you must learn his difficult

language full of inflections for another
self palpable as the stone in spoiled
fruit. Another self! The cheap
foundations of love shift—
before you always built in the quake-
proof plains where small rivers
pillow their heads in poplar
roots & turn all night
in the drought's persistent
insomnia. The cellar was dirt
still alive with roots
from which your father cut
your life in rigid board walls
incredibly steady
on the rippling floor of yellow
grain. In California, the cellarless
houses sway at the slightest
tremor.

At minus tide, the music
is deeper, gruff
music the retreating
sea makes in the rocks callused

with mussels you break
open for bait. The short
cuttyhunk bobs with its weight

on the limber twelve-
foot pole you poke in odd
sockets where eels
hold, tail in, to try whatever
the eclectic waves wash
through them. This music,
what more can you
catch, guess at, gummed down
by your small ration

of sense-news?
The pole is a parallel
to the horizon you lose as the opposite
earth pulls land from sea in fresh
creation. What custodian
fish will touch this index of another
world? You cannot reach the sea
by any step backward rigged

in clothes. The blenny eels imitate
kelp in its dwindling
from the land's foster-life.
Tenant body, you too rehearse your
constituent parts, your intervals

of utter jubilee.

TATTOO ARTIST

I'm the one who corrects the blurred
bodies, those grown uneven,
out of focus with
    loneliness, or, if mates
overlap— here a Noah's
    pair, there a hoax of incoherent

parts taught life. If you prefer
    some peculiar
blemish to attract
her love, I'll make a blue
    kiss nest in the hairy

armpit, or trace a little
    cupid like summer love's last
fly alighting
    on a nipple, transpose

rudely-done initials
    where a heart should
be. I can copy on your own
body whoever you really
    want: on your front her back

two-dimensional.
Her sex arranged around yours—
    you can put your pants on over
all four legs. No one will
know when you lean
    against her in the sub-

way, or at night submit
    both of you to careful
pleasure. In the mirror you'll relish
    the outline of her

buttocks on you
as you move but never
        see her face tattooed face-

down on yours.

III

FROM

String

1980

DELTA FARM

a friend weighs little
a wife makes the body heavy
as she swims away in the marriage
sheets— she seems more
strange than my mother's
face surfacing
in memory. so the drowned
displace the living—
not my wife's but
mother's thirst dries the sweaty

fingerprints
from the the handle of the short hoe
or cutter
bar skimming the overflow
our salty bodies deposit between
windrows. together we pressed

drool from the sugar
beets & threw
or wished to throw our bodies
like pulp to the few
hogs we kept for meat on the tufted
mud of an upstream
island. this is the sweetness we refused

one another.

      ◆ ◆ ◆ ◆

this neighbor is married
to solitude
another whose bridal sheets still smell
fresh drinks
greenish mouthsful from the cistern
children won't grow

up their roots churn in
the cultivated
zones fractured by a hundred
canal reflections.

· · · ·

when women visit
they only fix cots in fallen
down coolie shacks below
the town produce
sheds now abandoned & shifting
with the sun's weight.
when they leave boys

will lie restlessly
fishing in the narrow
beds skiffs make, between the pilings
hear the sheet
metal pop nails to trail
in a swifter river.

· · · ·

late November: a sixty-knot
squall through

the Straits breaks
levees, backs salt water miles
inland to preserve
what it kills. animal features
wake on bedroom windows—
buck deer the flood divorced;
our cow sewn with scars
bawls, against the dawn rubs
her painful ballast

of milk. my wife by instinct
washes her own
breasts before our daughter
feeds. birds in refugee dozens
scatter as I walk
a smaller yard. for days only boats

define the horizon. only the doctor
salt-stained
like us in boots & overalls
scares us. our daughter crawls
through fever one week
then her mother the week after

dies. my wife,
still my wife, what I have
of you, this residue, this love-

salt, will not let me cross private
places in my body
anymore. without you
I can only continue a snail inside
my shell of sleep trailing sticky
dreams. nowhere to walk I go
away from you.

      ◆ ◆ ◆ ◆

I am forty-two, my body
twenty-five.
my skin recopies over
& over my small daughter's

hand barely
holding against its current.
once I wanted to be still

water, a puddle the sky
fell in or the halo
my forehead molds from the saturated
marsh when I bend

my face to the first
unconfirmed rice shoot.
now I wait for the March-fed
river to clean
the delta, knead our thought-
out acres of orchard high
ground where picking ladders descend

legless into their own
reflections. the bottomland rice
is lost but these trees
reach deeper. rings of salt show
each step back the sea
takes. swaying from tree
to tree at last my daughter learns

to walk.

DIVINING

small world, the intricate
root protruding: imagination that makes
orchard trees
    so close they knit

inevitable distortion.
what then is the sky but delayed shadow
the eye a failing

    source of light?
after memory what leaf
won't seem faulty— witness poor van Gogh
at Arles sketching real
orchards until "ideas were the eyes
    of the eyes" & the dark of the mouth,

damaged night. overhead on my work-
shed the gross acacia
    crawls the metal
roof though I thin
it— the West is angular & cerulean
in the limbs where the bow saw
    still hangs teeth
up.

first speech— no begots, but
born of itself, starts:
the baby crawling the yard also
crawls "bird," "stick,"

or "tree." to be is to be raised
from mother-flesh plural,
to love distinction but be some part

of travail that summers
in an older body. Sara's grandmother
speaks as she walks
the sunburned orchard holding Sara:
these are the limits
& so is the way you repeat

them. you
drink this truculence; if you don't
choke you are healed.
sometimes it is only for a season
the eye must be a halo
for discolored April & you hold

back speech the way small carp
clog the irrigation
pump as it pants raising slough

water.

the urge to stroke the dead
    one back, hand-feed life
to the animal
body even as its soft
    vision dilates,
your calluses pulling
fur like lint from the unmendable

flesh. shake your head
    & coming back, hose the hutch
before your wife
six months pregnant sees

the rabbit. later
    she can launder your sweaty
overalls & empty the few
    black rabbit
pellets your pockets
caught. in the closet you

change & relishing the bachelor
scents of your underwear
    drop it to your father-in-law's
bathroom floor. now your voice

weighs nothing though
    you sing.

MILE HILL

December: the trees chafing.
instead of a hole
at the horizon the focused light
of a welder's torch: the sun

& the iridescent this-world fuse.
6 days' drive, Calif to the cramped Iowa
farms. by the roadside we stretch
as I explain where my family

grew. below,
small preserved Dubuque bristles
in 90's plain-face
brick across the uneven hills,
circles where the river does

south to slough water.
Sara picks up
snow; molds it to her small hand,
tinges it with her pink

flesh: concomitant beauty,
the bloodspot in the egg.
we are on our knees
every day to find on the ground
what we'd lost to the sky.

A RABBIT'S DEATH

the rabbit's spine must be snapped
by the left (thumb down)
hand as the right cradles the furious

body. the left hand, left
foot (gauche because
nonliteral & out of symmetry)

suffers with the disconsolate
humor of our species.
    what can the hand repent,
the eye
& mind abase? this rabbit's

death, this contagion blessed
by being altered to man
    who must die also
kicking? so fury apes gusto,

its gratuitous opposite.
    after the back legs are broken
at hock
one finger underneath can lift the skin
whole to be pulled
off entire with the twisted

head attached.

The Man Who Buys Hides

before I had a face
my mother supposed another horizon
aligned with that

wrong one contemporary hands fit
to relic Sioux.
maybe town behind the long
hills her brother's feed lot rode.
she was unmarried & wished

my face would never ripen
on the small stone memory left
of a necessary
lover. but I was born

white. & grew, bulky
& slow, never hearing my name
knotted in her tongue though
she must have sung

kneading father's pale
flesh, face to face drinking
distortion from each ripple
the other's body made.
or so I thought
when at night her lost
voice sounded the walls to the service
porch where at fourteen I dreamed
one pool dropping

to another hatchery trout threaded.
on the wall overhead
an exhausted
Jesus dried in milky shellac,

showing rain.

. . . .

summers I answered
her face surfacing in the bedroom
window to clean her eyes

or devotedly follow a crippled
hand through the word
"drink." my denim printed
blue sweat wherever I leaned
in her unquenchable

shadow. winters the ragged sky
my eyes folded as I slept
lost snow. the world formed under

our stamping feet & above it
breath drifted. with bare
hands uncle & I
shaped the cattle's frozen
noses, undid the ice their drool
tied through whatever
they ate. only the radio

spoke other names
when the lights were out
& eyes were adrift in their own

local winter.

. . . .

forty years later never thinking
of Dakota I still go faceless
into sleep & dream myself

intaglio under the animal carcass.
I never see the driver
of my truck as it weaves the dead
smells through the eucalyptus rows
swerving for potholes

in the gravel till the bones
give & under the tarp
the burst organs suck & squeeze.
what is death?
at the tail end they put one drain

at the other end they put
the tongue back in, intractable
& too big—
what can the doctor say

who is tired of his own body?

        • • • •

the poplar leaves go on multiplying
basic July. July sun
is swollen in the basin

where I cool
my drunken face. once I loved
my smell as I loved the hoof tipped
with stink trailing from the stud

barn. I have become a talker
in bars who wanted
to be only a handspan of red
earth trembling with ants.
Dakota stays under the washed
face even if Calif

turns it dark. only man is dumb

whose tongue shapes before the fingers
know. did these dead
animals talk
with hooves or with tactile
fetlocks praise
the grass as they stepped

off the limits of their hunger,
touching with their mouths
last? as I load each distended

body the winch
squeals, the cable cuts new
boundaries across
a piebald hide. only the head
drags & the eyes roll

over, counter to the earth.

no one knows the way out of his mother
except as she leads him
the final knot is his head
which drags the nerves
along the spine like doublestitch
up the reverse
of the body & outside the soft fabric
currents which pucker
erogenous zones. no other joy

but this string, this dorsal string
one end shit, the other end tongue.
who has not asked the way back?
who is not guilty of graceless longing,
& alone? watch that man who

puppet-dances through noon
traffic skinning light
off the chrome. though his hands
are broken his quarrel
goes on. his pants-front soaked, shamed,

he sings for pedestrians.
his mouth will bunch with old stitches
but he will sing, "privacy is only

contraction, heavy
body, dangle of shriveled nuts..."

DOG

after they had sewn him into the dogskin
they called him dog
as they had called him bird

    when the sky contracted.
to be human is to ache openmouthed—
the voice flapping, helpless.
can one say, without smiling:
    this is Gregor the peripheral

roach, a million years new,
& still hug man, dignify his pitiable daily needs
by existing in equal pain?
you would make yourself a dog

    first & pee openly, delighting
in this pliable flesh so cursed
with particular life that what seems gentle
    sweetens the flesh's repetition.

SOUP

a fistful
of spinach or chard sleep will make
a garden, & hidden snails that dying whistle

as the bunch opens, boiling: cautery.
temporary drunks, or just jobless
            you sing as envy cools—
one voice for bread, full of yourselves,
queued for bowls & the spotted

flatware I wipe & count
            as I give them out.
across Halsted a second
kitchen feeds the crippled, the old,
            those who never dry out

            who hum in common
speech Chicago, moan Chicago.
I'm the one I haven't counted
who won't eat from your bowl
though I wish humiliation for myself

            rather than anger.
each time, I go away undefined
though once I threw up—

breathing against my own fouled mouth
I asked you to forgive me
to stand aside as I knelt
sick with what I could not consume.

ARBEIT MACHT FREI *

his first day they asked
him to remove the swallows
so he hosed the mud
nests high up under

the sign while we watched, hats
off. once such ladders ran
out above a man's house
to touch frayed clouds.
now, a man is hired to wash the sky

or urge grass.
if you are uncomfortable in our world,
stop for a minute & put your eye
to the entrance hole, the swallow's
exit, hose pointed to another

nest. you look
inside: a woman is sprawled, legs
wide. you peer into her

hole too & see
a third hole or original
of your mouth hatching

the word "human,"
pretty feathers the spit
fades. press your face to the nest
& reach out with your liberated
tongue remembering
other words it kneaded into love
as many climb the ladder

* *"Work sets you free"*— *inscription*
on the gate at Auschwitz

behind you.
underneath, mud darkens

the tidy yard.
is that a guard kneeling
by a hole accidentally washed
from a nest? as he reaches down
the hole closes
over his ring finger.
this is how birds are made.

In Bosch's World

too we two are an odd detail
a man & a woman riding a fish
into the sky, too incidental to be

St. Anthony's temptation to carnal knowledge.
we refuse to look at each other
or at the scenes that encourage us

to suicide, ignore the street boys
beating a dead man's face,
the sum of carnal knowledge.

here men can have the faces of turtles
with the accuracy of hard practice.
all work on the body piecemeal:

one man develops the hand,
or accomplishes only *adductor pollicis.*
each is still only a piece of man;

this is the village, the first Chicago.
in such gestures as allegory permits,
guile is one-handed, but self-disgust

has cut off both its hands.
what made cities, *civility,* not even
kindness, is broken to fingerbones,

to nail parings a later man will realign
with tweezers, & with regret at the waste,
make only a handshake from the bones of two bodies.

we are leaving whatever way we can.
below, Anthony can go on kneeling
to his own demons, unable to cajole Jesus,

to make him fly. Anthony may want to be elsewhere,
he may want to ride the pony which
rubbed its saddle off on the bare wood

behind the picture; not to be a hero
or saint, to dream humble dreams
lit by the spit-sequins glazing

the pony's muzzle as the pony labors to be.
in this Hell vermilion masks the suicide's
face & habitual ocher the hero's backside—

the kind of hell we too could have made up
each alone.

WINGS

I am the carpenter called
three times in a dream drooled like resin
out of our marriage sleep,
who peeled the raw sun that bewilders

owls, who began with the birds
I pressed & dried as a child
in heavy nature books, who now ties
the angel's featherless arms

to this dreadful trellis.
yesterday's sky is also trained
to zones between the laths
as on each wing I work the truth

& doubt incised on our own hand-
prints. I want *truth* to repeatedly feather,
as in my dream, from the right—
but when I let the angel go

I want him to fly in ever tighter circles
with the stronger, more human, *doubt*
fanning our upturned faces.

PLANTING TROUT IN THE
CHICAGO RIVER

fishers of men
—Mark 1,17

because it is lunchtime
we lean from offices high over the river.
at a holding tank below the mayor
is on his knees as he mouths
the first fish coming down the hose.
his wife pulls back crepe
so aldermen & ethnic reps can help themselves

to rods as he then bends
over the awful garbage, as his lips let go
this fish rehearsed four nights
in which his tongue grew

scales, the Gospel epigram hooking
his mouth both ways
until he talked fish-talk
but still hungered for human excrement.
even in sleep he can will the river:
the midnight bridges folded

back for the newsprint freighter,
the Wrigley Building
wrinkling off the spotlit
water— he submerges a whole city

grid by grid to make one fish.
four nights he dreamt the different
organs for being fish,
but out of the suckhole soft
as armpit flesh a face always bobbed,
on the eyes a froth of stars.
in turn each of us

will have to learn to cough
up fish, queue from Lake St. Transfer
at the river to disgorge
& after, wade at eye-level

under Dearborn bridge, intuitive,
wanting flesh, wanting
the warm squeeze & lapse
over our skeletons because the fin repeats
fingerholds, the gills
have an almost human grin.

MAKING CHICAGO

We cannot take a single step toward heaven. It is not
in our power to travel in a vertical direction. If
however we look heavenward for a long time, God
comes and takes us up. He raises us easily.
                                    —Simone Weil

let it end here where the blueprint
shows a doorway,
where it shows all of Chicago
reduced to a hundred prestressed floors,
fifty miles of conduit & ductwork

the nerve-impulse climbs to know God.
every floor we go up is one more down
for the flashy suicide, for *blessèd man who*
by thought might lift himself

to angel. how slowly we become only men!
I lift the torch away, push up the opaque
welder's lens to listen for the thud
& grind as they pour aggregate,

extrapolating the scarred forms resisting
all that weight & think
the years I gave away to reflexive anger,

to bad jobs, do not count
for the steps the suicide
divides & subdivides in order not to reach

the roof's edge. I count the family years
I didn't grow older with the stunted
locust trees in Columbus Park,
the ragweed an indifferent ground crew
couldn't kill, no matter the poison.
now I want to take up death more often

& taste it a little—
by this change I know that I am not what I was:
the voice is the voice of Jacob
but the hands are the hands of Esau—
god & antigod mold what I say,

make me sweat inside the welding gloves,
make what I thought true turn heavy.
but there must be names
in its many names the concrete can't take.
what future race in the ruins
will trace out our shape from the bent

template of the soul,
find its orbit in the clouded atmosphere
of the alloy walls we used as a likeness

for the sky? the workmen stagger
under the weight of the window's nuptial
sheet— in its white reflected clouds
the sun leaves a virgin spot

of joy.

IV

FROM

Singing

1 9 8 5

SINGING

In grandma's nap the victrola skips
to Mimi's consumptive solo.
        Eighty-five, angina

pectoris crushing
her chest into the sheets,
she sings the thick Victor 78's

to herself, sings a husband
back, the horse's bite still smudged
blue above his collarbone
        where she would put her own lips

down, moaning.
        Only five, I leaned the door
closed & watched
her face shape over the unheard
while my mother called through

        the house below
that lemonade was with the others.
I won't answer,

I won't come back easily
from the close room, the only light
thrashed through a catalpa
branch as my cousins swing out

into July dark
defiant & greedy for pain.
        I am youngest of the youngest
daughter, Eve, who had neither voice

        nor moral sweetness.

I sing faintly
        in tune with the sleepers,
awed that no words
lie so well as the implied
melody we keep

in rhythm with our dead.

A Picture Of Okinawa

Out of adult hearing
the birds stammer this place
the animals intact
the remembered trees mismade
because a child painted them

from radio news & the interdicted
marsh back of Catfish Slough—
no GI drab but the Rousseau greens
snakes shed in their turnings

from heaven-held aquas & cerulean.
When the last Japanese soldier
gave up thirty years late
crashed down in some islander's

backyard, the sniper webbings cradling
his navel to the bandoliers
& commando knife with the four
metal knuckle-rings, I still looked
for my soldier uncle in this picture

my aunt never sent
to show how I imagined the enemy
condemned to eat close to heaven
the lonely madness for another's flesh,
his greenish waste wrapped in leaves

& stabbed on treeforks,
the mottled arm reaching for birds,
leaf by leaf making himself
innocent of his weapons—
only thirty years to come down human.

Bee-logic: each small life
for the hive,
but not one of them lived out

at the same speed—
your heart thuds *fortissimo* but slow,
my heart trots to its death.

Proto-druggist pickpocket or priest—
all begin as mysteries to themselves.
Big-Head Vincent who chews his pastels

& wipes spit with the blue
over his squat trees,
& Levonn too who wets himself

is one of us.
Our keeper Sister Agnes,
wrinkled as a peach-nut & left handed,

sings Latin, whose inside
is God's, she says, but we can go in
too with our tongues & the head

will follow, simplifying
heaven. Vincent went to heaven
in wet April. We sang a few words

of "Nunc Dimittis" among the gladiolus
& floribunda wreaths,
gripping each other's fingers

as we knelt all points in a compass,
expecting somehow to sing
Vincent up. But we belonged

to the headless Vincent
someone crayoned on the cloakroom
wall under his coathook,

the feet broken
right-angles, the heavy
arms straining against gravity—

a child's unfinished body,
waxy & insistent.

STUNG

to anger, a kind of species outrage,
I cursed & vowed to go back
at night when the wasps would cluster,
knot & re-knot into entropy.
Now I am alone

between the barn & the implement shed
for a long while looking up
but concentrating my polarity down here
feeling the planet turn

against human weight
its incredible friction showering off stars
which are the only other light

until just inside the shed I set fire
to a rag wet with cooking oil
I've wired to a long pole: it smoulders

then flares when I wave it
into webs as I inch the pole high
to the corner nest

iridescent with wings.
It's hard to do what the eye tells us—
coordinate the distant

fire as the long pole flexes
off bits of burning rag or bodies
(I can't distinguish)

& they fall among machinery,
illumine, close up, levers
& gears, a greasy differential
set down between sawhorses.

DRESSING GAME

After the men hunt,
the woman cleans the game.
She follows the puckered skin with a match
to burn off pinfeathers,
pushes & kneads squirrels from their hides,
printing against a haunch,

against the suddenly revealed
scraped breastbone, her live flesh.
Over the oiled underskin
her fingermarks, her scars,
the thick crown of a wart,

maybe a hair between her flesh & theirs.
The knife-nick will be cooked in,
the touches-for-nothing.
Even the trash organs

pick up her image as she sorts,
breaking the membranes, turning the joints
180 degrees to break their lock
on remembered fields,
burrows & slide-holes in burdock.

Afterward she soaks in the stream—
the red curling off,
the current clotting around rocks.
She lets her soiled shirt fill,

removes it & wrings it. & her pants
as she swings them,
emptied of herself, fill too with a clear
though invisible body
which passes, shivering the denim, back
into the stream.

CUTTING OUT A DRESS

Sara's fingers will find the way
before her eyes do
in the river of print-goods daubed

with human figures.
At thirteen she lays out
a world to fit her imagined body
in the attic room held
by its yellow light high in the treetops.
Every night she sheds into the outside

animals her childhood taught:
no panda nor hippogriff,
but Jake our setter run down by a car,
a snail popped underfoot,
a sluggish fly tapping
out its life between two panes—

each death a kind of rhythmic moulting,
a forgiven pain
her scissors briefly isolates.
In the bedroom below, my wife
& I each think we wrestle
a different angel as we shake

& pant in an unbreakable marriage-hold.
The floor above us trembles—
the sewing machine
thumping the same cloth over & over.
The pulse is threaded

into the arm-linked humans
repeated to infinity—
a life so simple its seamless embrace
could be skin itself.

A Letter To Ron Silliman
On The Back Of A Map Of The
Solar System

I weigh 486 lbs on Jupiter
    I can't tell you why
I am crying why
        whole ridges of the memory
pull loose this immense
gravity keeps us down
under the slide I discarded first
    my old father who weighed more
here on my back a smaller hump somehow
my penis came out
        wrong or a strangely distended
heart girls touch for luck I threw
        down my weapons too what use
I said poor Aeneas is the afternoon
when distance turns our atmosphere
to frozen gas & shadows the gods give
        a discernible half-life
winks by the best
of our instruments the father
Jupiter ate the most promising
    of his children the Latin myths say

little they were not grateful
to the sly Greeks a fallen
    city was given curiously foreign
buildings with supports constructed
    on heavenly principles Cassandra
for instance screamed & the water-clocks
ran faster in our color bands
    sodium insects & our smaller
life take on radiance &
become explosive when it rains we know
it is a warning
    do not even cry the atmosphere

is unstable keep it under sawdust wet
with oil the moist armpits & loins
    are unstable for our use only
the subtle dust that drifts
    down when the last of the fallen memory
settles & Jupiter surrenders
a final disguise for our mothers
    were raped & we grow up half-gods in turn
to eat or forget our real origins

SABOTAGE

expresses the self you'd rather spoil
than give, a forfeit,
to the enemy— or even to a brother,
who might say, as mine did: *kneel,*

I want to see polish on yr lips.
I remember bobbing to kiss
his sneakers which I had polished

as a joke for a cousin's wedding.
I was eleven, but now
foot-fetish is a term I associate
with whitey's arrogance to play blackface,

or with subordination of desire,
wanting to kill, but instead
incorporating the enemy
in a literal sense like the cannibal arachnid

wrapping its misinterpreted young.
For years I wanted a gothic revenge
like the one I imagined
for the black shoeshine jockey at the Randolph
subway stop. Mid-sleep, my head vibrating

against the window of a late night local,
I thought the black man's power
when he went down on his knees

to polish, caress, rub his spit
into the stranger's shoe.
I imagined him
humming to it under the storefront neon.
The shoe would go up near his mouth.
He dropped, dribbled all he'd held back,

caught it again
in the blackening, scrubbed it to a liquid,
with his palm worked
the leather, skin to skin, feeling

how the human welt followed the shoe welt.
With one finger he kept the pulse
moving, going up the man's leg—
the color climbed with his hand,

the polish darkening the other's skin
past the sock edge up,
shining the light hairs
until the stranger flesh was like his—
soft, the whole body dozing
in symbiotic rhythm with his, darker,
the sheen & sweat even coating an insect

which closed like a knot in one polished eyefold.

II   Other brothers fight. My own sons so knotted into
complementary musculature that their quarrel—
who'll feed our ratty chickens— becomes a prob-
lem
in geometry. Until the older hurts the boy who's
crying now. I splash all the water from the bucket
on them.

And explain how not to fight. Explain Konrad
Lorenz's gander Paulsen: say chickens fight or don't
fight the same way. They won't let themselves kill;
they sabotage their own urges in rapid, stochastic
penance. Beak wide and ruffed larger, the dominant
one interrupts itself mid-charge to chase an imag-

ined enemy to the side of the weaker chicken. Or the
weaker pretends to feed or be distracted by some-
thing, something it won't eat mixed in the shit and
fallen food.
It will not fight, but it knows only this way to
submit.

Karl, our Chicago friend, for example, who lay his
head near a D-8 tread to stop the construction at
Diablo Canyon. If the slowed machine had gone on,
the friable clay tread castoffs dropping as the
machine shuddered, stopped several head-widths
away? The red-faced driver screaming: if he would
have had a Goya beak and the goggled-eyed Goya
owlishness of *¿No hay quien desate?*, who would've
withstood his attack?

Karl called it *liability*, the Christian peace a man
gives his enemy when he excuses the belligerent
from a death that won't hold them both.

Protesting the death penalty as he had protested
the ITT in Chile, the draft and Nixon's Cambo-
dia because guilt is indivisible no matter how
many dead, Karl walked eight days to the state
capital carrying a ½-scale electric chair, strapped
to himself a weight he couldn't put down to
enter a car. By the time he got to the vigil, it was
a cat's-cradle of 2 x 2's & wire, a device, a con-
ductor of rage. Cars ran him into the roadside
weeds, the splintered colonizing bindweed, the
troubled fire, pyracantha, whose berries draw
small birds to the thorns. Was he the fool I
called him? Were the few dozen people who
went into his campaign, walked with him in

relays, his fools? We were so embarrassed we
didn't pledge. I quarreled with my wife three
days, and so we didn't drive to meet him at the
first overnight farm town. We didn't walk. Was
his a displacement activity? The sideways walk,
the cramped stasis I see in the boys' wrestling, the
one's blood melting into the chaff and rice-hulls
a single foolish hen pecks at between their shoes?

NEWS

The *Chronicle* "Green Sheet" dries out
BIC pen mustaches & goggles,
underwear women
the boys decorated with paisley lesions,

interpreting the news.
Extinction seems a protracted, ironic task:
though Hitler's
manager Albert Speer dies

only a few pages ago,
I remember Hitler's death
on the radio was the work of an age,

a whole industry;
Eva Braun was anybody's sister gone wrong.
Finally I go on my belly
with the children to highlight

what is real. Newsprint bruises
ripple all over me;
faces come off on my sleeves

as I sweat & fill
page after page, call for new stacks.
Captions pull off like scabs,

but reversed:
this news understood only in mirrors,
accepted by the body,

will teach me shame.
My wife kneels too
on what we once thought important:

boldface sex crimes,
ferocious nations & burned-down discos.
Unaware of all they carry,

both boys stagger
in with old *Trib* issues,
the *Guardian, The Berkeley Barbs*

so yellow from garage weather
that they flake & snow
down on us lost, unrecoverable lives.

THE COAL BIN IMAGINED FROM MY GRANDMOTHER'S DESCRIPTION

as she gives me the scuttle
& snaps the light cord at the top of the stairs,
means it is so far down that I must fall

headfirst, which I do,
my aim, until I reach this remote earth,
taken from stories children agree to,

wanting ghastly secrets.
But the beasts that happened after my words
to make them were only the kind of horse
or dog a fat first-grade pencil draws,
hardly able to manage their own gravity—

their eyes, dots heavy from lifting blackness.
& so I discover what coal is, how slow—
I pick a lump & think I feel fronds,
or a paw-print pressing back

my own blackened hand.
I go into the room-sized bin—
here I build a campfire
to begin to make the way back.
The first step is to re-invent everything,

to domesticate what I imagined,
to bring light out of all that scribble.
But the weight of the dark

flattened cups & a canteen almost half-gone,
flattened even my pockets.
The horses couldn't breathe.
They knelt & rolled until their curves

gave out against one another.
I looked into the eyes of one dog
& saw his black vision go dense

from the inside,
the pupils of his eyes mold
over my face reflected backwards,
that crooked grin knotted over my thumb

as I sucked comfort & cried.
It took years to give up questions,
to let the species go crippled.
Now at last I'm almost happy
with the blackness though I still live

with you, poor horses caught in implication—
if only I had an eraser to rub over
your fuzzy muzzles,
if only I could wipe the black-flecked drool.

GILL BOY

for John, my son

The toys I bought for you
splash down in your brothers' tub,
are rubbed paintless,
protean, in the 15 yrs coming down:

the space vehicle Apollo,
the rubbery aliens,
& the tooth-scarred astronaut
who trails air-hose,
prepared to go breathless

into the child's world.
You lived only five days,
unable to surface, cyanotic

in the isolette, then cold—
the way I've learned to accept you
when I wash your two brothers real,
when I shape each

of their small parts over
& over again with soap.
I tried to forget, to sublimate,
but under seven inches of bathwater,
out of reach,

you learned to breathe.
The suds your brothers leave,
the soapy waste,

webs galls & scaly eyelets
all over your skin
so cruel no one could love you

& want to survive.

ATTIC

Mice, their eyes studded
by a 40-W bulb

or barn swallows spread out against
one small hole, tearing

themselves to get in.
I'm belly-down on splintery board

without a shirt, balancing over rafters.
Sometimes up to my wrists in cellulose

& rat-dirt, I touch *National
Geographic*s or the cardboard violin-case

webbed to 2 x 10's, scrape the bloodied
overhead where I have to writhe

to get under while my wife
below, the ceiling plaster sounding

between us, syncopates then re-does Chopin's
Black-Key Étude. I change

hands when she does, sweating
at the *forte*; in tandem we release

one hold for the next
in my secret crawl to the cupola.

Every time I see more as I stand,
the cupola's shutters one by one

ascending my face until my eyes
are clear: a kind of helmet

I grow into, the outside laddered,
inimical. The music ripples through me.

LUCKY TIGER

The driver counts us
by twos, the gloomy with the prescient,
    fat by thin: not one
wants to see out.
They want to push their legs straight,

    try a near body fit
to the stranger, rock
away as the bus downshifts to turn
out of the area of boarded stores,

massage parlors where the implied
    corrects the real.
My handkerchief is spread
over the greasy seatback,
    over the correlative
odor of pomander

orange in my aunt's closet,
    its acid dissolving
the sweaty darkness where I hid
as I hide now
deliberate in pretend sleep
    my face turned
to a world distorted by another greasy

headprint on the window.
I slept & the same years slept
    secret, scratched.
From the closet I barely hear
my older, slow cousin corrected, his hand
    I sense guided—
chew this bread he says to himself

chew, & as I knew he would, rubs

the greasy part in his hair
before he molds the sticky approximates,
alphabetical animals I who already knew
        how to read taught him.
Bite Denny he told the animal he rubbed

        near my mouth.
This still stands for that:
        his urine smell, the Lucky Tiger
my aunt stroked into his hair,
her hand shining from the contact
with him, her voice
        implying love.

1942

Treelevel night, innocent of planes—
hot night, mildewed
Iowa dawn a few hours above the porch.
Down by the slough something snaps

through brush or eats,
snout down in fur & loose matter.
I want to come back to the *Photoplays*
& mystery novels rotting

inside the cottage's sawndown chiffonier,
the summer's-only smells,
involve every sense in what I was—
not caring whether I am
predator or the one fed on,
but connected as they are by a chemical reaction,
make the dark crawl

to the watering place,
that one indefinable sense
singing in vibration with the other's pulse.
I can bring back the Chicago dance-band,

the Philco's indicator more red,
as the sound grows
& is cut mid-song by louder war news.
When I concentrate I can feel
the slippery 12-gauge as I sweat against its stock,
waiting for birds;
I can bring back the smell

of my father's
long-johns knotted on a towel-bar,
the tick of the midges
burned up in the Coleman lamp,

celestial, short-range lives whirled by the heat
of mistaken desire—
but I can't bring back all the senses at once,

not even one body entire:
one midge, nor anything as big as
my younger sister sweating out fever,
her hair caught in a bunk spring

as she thrashes to escape
whatever predator doubles her body heat.
The night she died I lay on the bunk above,
trying to draw in the music,
dilate with the radio's ruby eye,
my mouth forming as the doctor

cooed instructions to her,
& then to my parents to take me
to their room where I lay in what I could
remember of her position
& exhaled the longheld remainder of her song.

V

FROM

Eden

1989

INSTRUCTIONS FOR FISHING THE EEL

for Ray Carver

December pools, latent, crosshatched
    in low wind
& the rest of the stream all exegesis.
Steelhead will nose
the water-seams around rocks
    where you can drop

yarn-flies or a roe-dip compound
    that bleeds red taste
around your hook,
    the fog head-high & bleeding too

out of nearby firs
hooked down by the same ice
    you sometimes pull through your reel
in stiff, small O's that mean
    you've lost all weight

at the line's end: your connection,
    your tie to the it-world.
Your second lesson: when a fish
twists, leaps through

to our world to throw hook
    or die, contention stops—
where the line enters water
    is equipoise,
centering: fish & human at last
    in balance & glorying,

if either can, in the other.
& last lesson: the steelhead's context
    is ocean; the hardest
lesson is to let go

what one can't be, first immersing
	the releasing hand,
dirtied by bait
but dry enough paradoxically to slime
	off in rainbows
the fish's protective coat: the hand's

reward is to feel
the no-shape of water, feel human warmth
drain away in the wetting.

BIRD-WATCHING

Across the channel, Mare Island welders cut
bulkheads & winch up
riveted slabs of the WW II

mine-tender. I can see
the torches flash against visualized rust;
I can see so far
back that the war cruelties are camouflaged

as feats of scruple.
The binoculars sweat rings around my eyes,
& when my arms tire, it's the sky that comes down

fuzzy through the Zeiss
10 x 40 lens into debris— the shoe, paper news
& condoms, the"beauty

from brevity derived" I can't catalog.
I'm on the flyway for marbled
godwits, scoters & loons,
but taxidermy might have devised what I think

is only a dead heron peppered with grit,
marshgrass poking
out the bird's buggy eyeholes.
I want to get down,
include myself in the focus: the war,

all epithets, between memory & present things
memory can't yet reach.
Though the marsh is a constant

madras-bleed between old soda bottles
that slash grids in the earthbound
walker's boots & the heuristic dieback

of the grass, I'm on one knee
to this Bird-in-the-volleys-of-lesser-birds,
praising glut but lifting
binoculars once more to distance myself

from it. Idolatry begins in one's fear
of being the only thing, saying, for example,
to detritus, *let it linger, let even just the feathers*

of it stay— that is why I pick
up my glasses with the little men still in them.
They are so intent on forgetting;

they are so self-contained & innocent,
lit both by the binoculars' small
circles of sky & by the torches the men stroke
against the steel that arches over them.

HARNESS

26 years married luckily
each to the other's eros, you & I,
but our friends who married

only for context
or for patience with a sexual prey
find desire an irresolute

prayer that weeps for itself.
Not a Lamia, not small Keats's lack
by which she was made hungry for men—

even a woman who loved women,
the 20's painter Romaine Brooks,
drew humans in disciplinary blacks
evolving out of animals

in the lower parts of their clothes.
Each seems open to the trespass—
they're like the thieves in Dante's hell

who forever change
from humans to beasts to humans they've affixed
themselves to because they have

no sense of self.
Does one give up to fury for love
equal to it & go lost

into somewhere black
as the IRT station, led by the other's surrender
like the woman we once saw guiding
her blind husband by clinging to a harness

of canvas she probably made,

in tandem going down the subway stairs,
steering him around dogshit trampled

into incipience,
the loose floor tiles,
the dangers she must become impetuous for—
just barely before the uptown train rockets

to them, the wife slaps
down his endangered arm.

GOOD FRIDAY

First the procession representing
what could destroy us,
then the flagellants raising welts on one another
in praise of it—
then, *hosanna*, the warty New Mexico gourds,

the strings of chilis.
My Volvo is out with the other Volvos
absorbing the weak New Mexico spring—
it's OK to shuffle for a while
with the agnostics because the white-
faced Death who tinkles

a soft bell ahead of Jesus
calls everyone to step in the walk
past embarrassments of booth-sweets & tourist
rosaries: this Death
for whom maracas knock

wears plastic huaraches under his muslin
shroud spotted with candle-wax.
Then, finally, the four enter in robes, swaying
with the advertised Cristo

Crucificado, red & grainy piñon,
borne on 2 x 4s, the wool of his knitted scalp
catching on splinters.
I'm by the entrance
to belief where cripples groan

deeper into whatever genetic
twist to kiss a photographed Jesus—
see across the placard their wet kisses

step, bleaching details

from God's face. They carry a Jesus so heavy
that their knees buckle in the dance—
their art is grief
so complex in its steps that the young
falter & the old go down

thrashing in the telepathic spill.
If not one of us is healthy,
yet we try to sing,
as those to whom I'm joined now
hand to hand sing against my mental defect

that won't let me roll
as the uniformed Daughters of the Sacrament
roll, their capes sluicing on the tile floor.

Driving With One Light

that strokes shapes out of the trees,
that makes far-back animal eyes
prickle, I fight right
then left the two halves of an S-curve

four hours into the Sierras.
I keep the white
centerline flowing under the VW,
denying the peripheral

animal world that flares momentarily.
I'm in a second world
the radio makes because sleep presumes

that first world I will not to enter.
Wrong-faced signs reflect my only light
as the two-lane road overtakes

rockface turn, then tree then tree.
In the right-hand dark something lives,
spreads against the windshield,

then breaks through
to where I am, civilized, wary & cursing.
I flap my arms as the creature flaps

in the glass shards.
Tree patterns come into the light,
then trees as the car skids,
parting laurel & low brush

I oddly try to name
before the car stops, tearing a visible blaze
in a big Doug fir.
Whatever it is is across one leg

as I roll out the sprung door;
it moves, it flutters as I push
my back against the door,
trapping inside the worst I can imagine—

nothing so simple as a feathered self,
nothing so arcane you couldn't make it out,
least light, in you.

HALLOWEEN

But the costumes won't come off—
beast face,
or the skeletal kid whose mom lipsticked

on his pimpled midriff
a working stomach
& lungs so real he had to hold his breath

twice not to inhale
pee-marks & the dumpster smell
through alley shortcuts

& past hard-hat bars.
Now you sidle past pimps' Rivieras
& pink LTDs, animal life

barely cool in the animal
skin seats the got-up girls warm
as they echo in fatigued mews

the long riff of cat-scream
gaudy love
could blare when you're caught

in the body wild to lay down
your muzzle,
your hair on end, witless,

against another pelt.
Out of the neighborhood,
middle-class porchlights blue

the jungle dark.
Go in through the hinged dog-door,
pawing a grip on linoleum to lie

where Lawrence Welk or
Honeymooners reruns soothe some grandma
or widower grandpa lonely &

moaning with the Welk brass section.
This is how you learn *human*
until the ends of the lyric tangle

in your long ears,
& the TV is off, the picture pinched
down to a dot.

Then pad haltingly after the halting
other you'll replace as he or she limps—
like you soloing on hind legs,

not quite human still, but trying, trying.

THE POUR

Four of us men by twos
lug the 20-gallon
meltdown kettles in step
with the glowing

kettle ahead,
our company coveralls
flowering spills
& then burn marks,

our heavy shoes crusted
with sugar magma we'll pour
smoking in the cold
spread-room

where the "spread" girls
choir sweet
damns, greased gloves up
as they back for us

tight to the walls
("peanut-brittle"
was Nov. when "mayonnaise"
shut down).

I prayed after twenty
carries for flu,
my forearms twitching,
prayed all night

as I steered
the bulky kettle to the tables
with my partner's body.
God talked

to me in the toilet
about the girls,
the old one who spits
into the sizzle before

she calls it names
of her man whose knob
she wants burned
off before she ends her shift.

But I urge & I urge God
for the flat-nosed girl
with the sugar blister
in the V of her uniform

she shows as she bends,
devoted to the pour.

CLIMBING SEARS TOWER

"Stuntman Daniel Goodwin, dressed in a
Spiderman outfit, climbs the west face of building,
using suction cups and metal devices, in 7 ½
hours . . . is arrested after ascending the 1,454 foot
building."

New York Times, 5/26/81

4 hours into the climb,
you're still in a reflected Chicago,
against the reflected downtown
grid of older buildings, hardly discernible

humans mirrored close
to your cheek on the breath-wet glass.
Or maybe you imagine humans,
imagine their small concerns

after some time trying.
The sky comes
onto the glass some floors later;
it includes a TV copter

you don't turn to see
examining you, wanting the arachnid
change TV will show as pathos.
You sweat across a divided sun

into the out-of-focus
western neighborhoods where I imagine
the Douglas el rattling
past my window on Leavitt, sucking

curtain against the rusted screen—
instead, the copter camera
shows fatigue-points a wiseass announcer
superimposes on your back

as though you're holding Humboldt Park
like a bandage over racial turmoil.
He looks for human
failure, for regret not exhaustion—

as the bartender switches to the Cubs
& miming a spider scurry,
clears lunch glasses, olives & chorizo

scraps into a basin.

STERNO

squeezed, rag-strained for the waxy
alcohol,
sipped for mortal fire:
the coatless man drinks it,
tasting equally rapture

& *a priori* death,
his few teeth coating & his breath,
when he swallows it,
burning down to mere appetite

for more breath.
Crying out, having put his tongue to it,
he is immune
like the literalist porcupine

at last free to eat the toad
he's surprised himself by catching,
devouring first the toad's poison

gland, lathering his face toxic.
The man thrashes
the wet municipal lawn, rolls
against a camphor tree
the rain has thrashed into perfumed

wakefulness, coating
but not diluting his man-smell
for the park cop who hunkers
over him, a nightstick's length away,
his leather cop-harness creaking
as he flicks snails
off the sweet creases in the man's face.

Zoo

In its envy, the white-bibbed okapi tramples
the peacock— over the clay
the stutter of its hooves, all expletives.
That's why the boy is let go

by moonlight, charms glued to his chest,
into the grass-eaters-of-the-African-veldt corral.
Naked, savage for their cure,
he scares a pygmy oribi that's clearing mimosa

rubbish from the watering trough
with its muzzle.
As it runs, khaki then
umber in the little light, it coughs
& coughs feathery mimosa

blossoms; the boy won't go after, but in turn
drinks out of the trough
clogged mouthsful. Slowly, then, he tracks

in the tracks, his feet tender,
past the padlocked feed bins where a one-bulb
glow makes the straw a brocade.
He'll let the stopped antelope sniff,

let it lick mimosa drool
from his lips as he tries to assimilate
through each link in the food chain

empty anger that like sex
is the ache for absent parts the other has.
Another night he'll cure

the lazy meat-eaters, stand
for man, in thought's brothel find his ecstasy,

so afraid urine drops muddy
on his leg, his ribs clawed with his own hands.
He'll let them nip him,

let fang or claw drag
the hairless interstices of his body.
Only those trapped between the literal

& an appetite— these he can't help:
the greedy mouse a whole week caught in poultry wire
goes on growing, one half *head*,
the other half *rosy-anus-in-fur-threads*—
the wire opening closed on its middle,
it eats in the emu's pen & defecates

in freedom.

with Spock ears & a snout
incongruously mixed, & the other child his mother
& I pretend not to know,
who came home as a tree, bark lapped on

like feathers— both their bodies
are so closely zipped,
buttoned, or sewn into the bizarre

that the bodies can't fall apart
in sleep. The younger one's in bed
with the inked-on leaf veins still crawling
his hands as I talk

from his brother's bed opposite:
it is Oct. 31 everywhere
& there are no children because
we must do what the costumes tell us—
adults must live

to extinction in Jordache or Izod casuals
while kids have feathers or fur,
& they eat the meat-threaded wind

from burger-stands,
cursed with an appetite for grass.
To tell my sons more, I must make the '40s
Riverview Park & around it nighttime
Chicago, literal but dissolving in neon lather:
we're on the 80 ft. hump

one's head takes before the stomach follows
Dead Man's Curve
& the roller-coaster cars dive
again into gravity.

You hear screams best under the structure,

your forehead against a cool girder,
your bladder tight with Orange Crush or beer,
believing in alone
though there must be a dozen other pissers
in the dark around you, & that colicky moan

each gives dopplers to a metal-on-metal
group screech as the train passes,
& in the overhead bars of light
you see paint flecks
snowing: the structure bearing up all the orbits

shivers but stays.
Ignore all this, the Parachute Jump,
Giant Wheel, but be drawn in your listening
to the carousel where animals
once danced their limited steps around

a march tune's 3-minute circuit,
& now you see only humans
on poles prancing for their riders
the intricate human round

of gestures— you must ride them,
selecting your parents by what you want to be,
riding, your furry thighs
tightening at the percussion parts

of the song, your hearts accelerating
until you sleep.

THE GRAND EGRESS

was Barnum's way to stir
believers, usher them out before they gave way
facing the wolf-faced boy
along the clogged path to the next tent,

their dimes already gone & the boy growling
what could be words.
TO THE GRAND EGRESS Barnum's sign with an arrow
said, as though some fresh

atrocity, on its haunches, waited.
So believers left the boy's world before grief
at the differences between them
overcame joy at their likeness.
My brother's joy was to guide me

past dangers, the detours child-logic
cuts through fences
the long way to school, Iowa snow painting out
unpaved walks, even the ERIE RAILROAD & SOO LINE
escutcheons on the boxcar sides
of the 75-car freight stopped as far as

our wheel-level eyes could look.
& snow melting on the still-hot tracks.
Trains could be on the spur
past class-bell sometimes, past our short legs'
strength, wavering, as Joseph Campbell says,

before the absolute.
Religions, he goes on, make the way to dying
grand as Barnum's exit come-on
so that no one would linger here

loving the animal, capitulating.
Gerry & I blocked by a long freight,

breath-beards condensing on our mufflers.
Stooping, we saw snow on that side

as on this, & old footprints.
Dirty ice hanging from the couplings
& behind the wheels,
studded with gravel & cinders the wheels threw.
It won't move, Gerry said, scrambling,

gratuitously dropping a book, bending again
under the wheel for it.
From the other side, he leaned & looked
across at me, looked, not a boy at all.
Hell, I wanted to go under,
I still want to go under.

Instructions For Rowing

across the reflected sun the skiff cuts
should include diagrams
of the radius joint of the wrist,
a kind of human oarlock.
The island in his head the sweated rower looks at

is sublime in a way
the island one can't face to row to never is:
so deliberately choose a distant

mark to go away from—
this is the way to go straight

to what you can't face. Your father's distant
cousin drowned rehearsing suicide,
& the fish you think of eat

under his clothes
(your wrists ache already)—
but this is your *mother's* cousin's island.
The scoured paint-cans

for berrying & your brother's little weight
hold all this in balance.
& balance is somewhere in the ear
a fish doesn't have.
The water which substitutes for thought

runs inaudible through the fish.
It senses its world full-length:
its balance is the dark nerve-matter along its spine
aligned to the imagined horizon.
How different a boy is

consuming father's cousin in a joke
to scare younger brother,

who wails & won't look into the muddy swirl.

Pause when no current corrects the skiff.
You are there
when willow roots tangle your oars;
the back of your head will brush through the trailing

branches the inside of your head saw.

MATTHEW'S LESSON

fails, yet the piano learns the music
a 10 year-old wants
to make: this difficult June

the fingers pace into,
counting rhythm with the heart or breath—
I hear it through the roses

that I weed outside his practice room.
Separating the bermuda
grass's successive, fugal nettings
from rose thorns,
my fingers inattentively rub
pain as his rub song— I have blood-dots

on my wrists & dirt
from which I take blood-smell.
The music stops
as my fingers find the roots,

the earth pulling back
at my pull. Matthew, I know, is listening
for what I hear as I listen,
as quiet as I can be

to the process the Bach exercise
posits because silence
is not an evasion but a challenge the musician
dares—each of us listens

on his side of the open window.

CATFISHING

is best hot July midnights,
stars catching on a ragged
horizon the willow-lined slough makes,

the Coleman light
coloring nearby berry canes green.
The crawfish traps dry out,
crawfish pieces
still crusted to the wire netting

crawfish consciousness fought through—
what can a 12 year-old know,
what do I teach
in teaching Paul to crack them
& pull the hook-barb against

the snarled little flesh & leave them
living to go again over
the uneven slough floor?
Catfish eat anything

with a hard-lipped smile—
Paul should learn all
I don't want to teach him,
should imagine crawfish pain & the steel

in him teaching him sideways
moves in the ooze he can't imagine
until I show him how
to handmold the local favorite
bait: deliberately dirtied blood

& meal, the chicken guts
three days in a jar.
Mosquitoes knot along his arm;

he twitches the rod,
properly hoping to catch nothing.

BLUE

Reroofing first our shed's south,
weather-burned slant,
I lever up by pairs the crumbly cedar shakes,

the sun that's annealed to the roofing nails,
while I breathe in rot,
insect casings & incidental dirt

that puffs black under my pry.
On my knees, I dance back from vertigo
until for balance I must put my eye

down to the splintery hole
I've accidentally broken, & with that one eye
drop through shelves, tool clips,

& so many coffee cans of nails
that they rust
what light the hole draws down.

I'm dizzy but resist memory that tastes,
thing by thing, love's famine.
When I pull my eye back from the hole,

the things by their gravity stay
the absolutes our family kept
negotiating: against Fran's temper,

put her immutable black-sheep status;
for the X-mas cards
trussed but never sent (1968),

give shelves of home-canned cukes going
green a second time.
I bob & twist to look away,

slivers cross-stitched into my knees
& up the gloves I slap
& paw through, compensating—

I hang on at last only by looking away,
only by relacing with my eye
the garage wall's clematis against

the down-there— by eye hanging, for example,
the drying laundry, sock to contiguous
shirt to shirt, concentrating

every way I can to make fit the last piece,
our tied-back puppy who on two legs
nips the Levi's hung crotch up: blue

flows out of the sky into them.

THE SPIDER

All a March week I watch,
stopping the fretsaw,
spilling brads & the birdhouse

pegs, watching the spider
caress a braille of light-dots,
no-weight angles
of the victim-eater paradigm

I deny as I too build, my hands
all encysted slivers & hammer-bruises,
for song the finches repeat

to their own images, the counter-birds,
in the garage-shop windows
they fly at, tapping, turning aside
from death only by looking to the trees.

But my look won't lift,
& my song is to myself as the very small

birdhouse hole tightens around me.
Each day the sun slides
later on the window toward a web

more comprehensive.
So I sand the grainless pine parts, align jig
for glue & the pin-small brads,

relishing each task,
even indecorously eating at the bench,
wanting to finish when the spider does.

LADDER

Head at sill-level,
she looks back into her bedroom,
out of reach: her school clothes
the plump Hummel kids,
the posters bellying out from moist

August walls.
The outside stucco rasps
her toes, rasps knuckles
she thinks are big
when the chain fire-ladder
sways & she goes down by feel

into adult illusion,
to watch her parents in their window
kiss TV kisses past the 10 P.M. news,

sleep into the late show she's denied.
Her fingers numb in the flow of chain.
Neighbors' lights ripple
up her pj's as she comes legs first

down into the yellow & mistuned taupe
that flares around the actors.
If she could lean through
the window's initial cool to that
burning they pretend

to endure, she'd speckle
with love-sweat too.
Now she noseprints the glass;

she's twisted up in ladder,
aching all over
to lip-synch a love she can't yet hear.
She doesn't know the sound

is off; her mother has let go
her sleeping father's hand—
each of them is adrift
in real life so prolix with echoes
that suffering
blazes out of each word love could say.

In the drafty Kiwanis hall
still hung with V-E Day bunting,
my mother, your sister, pounded out
"Addio, del passato" for you, Violetta-

dying-to-manipulative-love.
The senior judge, a voice coach, grunted
& shifted in his folding chair
as you lifted your hands to the fleur-de-lys

stamped metal ceiling,
crying inadequately but believing yourself.
Five rows back, I must've looked
up, Violetta, from my Marvel

comic, thinking myself that Marvel hero
so wounded that medicos had condemned each
of his bodily processes separately—
inside his mask a face so hideous,

so amorphous from the lab accident
that only the mask held it together
(each spangle an actual bolt-head),

the blue mask hiding blue skin—
like you a victim,
not a weak Alfredo I couldn't understand.
In the front row, three other Violettas,

their heads worked in duplicate
nineteen-forties' finger-curls,
turned as I suddenly coughed

& bled on the comic pages.
Even my occult ability to constrict the atoms
of my body at will couldn't stop

a simple nosebleed.
After the audition my mother raged—
but who is to say we two had no right

to try to suffer, to grow into detail,
sotto voce imitate better singers
dying, each of us pretending so hard
that the notes come out bloodstained,
though not song.

So High

that you can see where you fell
from the Dunkerton silo
    at nine, or the sumac spear
I aimed at you,
threatening your eye— the retrospect
    is all the way

to childhood— you're riding the sway,
each foot cupped
    in last year's scions,
sawing, sawing a place for the sun

to freckle onto the roses.
    My role is brake
on the nylon line I've tied to my waist,
a Möebius-twist that loops

yellow through the camphor
    tree's eternal green. Bark comes down;
then you scab off a bootheel
    like some body part,
always pulling more line until I lose
what I knew of you.
    One tree's enough

logic to climb through imagining
    veer under the elbowdeep green,
taking countless
false handholds until you come out

in sky. Now the sun multiplies
    off your tools,
but you won't ripple the saw again
    through the steady groan

of the wood— you've seen the horizon
    cut by roof-peaks
in your balkanized neighborhood of small lots.
    In identical trees you see
other men sway
    over reflected heat thrown
up from the asphalt shingles: you wave

they wave.

    for my brother, Gerry

EDEN

*"I am very young & ye are very old
wherefore I was afraid."*
—Job, XII

Sprinklers spot the patio
edges, spot the rest-home piano which gives
us Scarlatti or 40's

show tunes but means heaven is not denied
even the reluctant,
those so old they'll have to die twice.
As my wife goes on playing,
seedpods smack
& flatten out under chair-wheels:

around us is a garden
so choked & many-minded that size
is a function
of reconciled disregard.
Ebullient suckers twig out after

ten feet of desperate trying,
their leaves half-clenched
but green. Behind poked-out screens,

inside the rest home,
something even older hums
back— replete, unanimous in the music
my wife uses to call them:

burr-faced grandpas
so inward they are almost amoebic,
the grandmas in lumps under sheets—
the bed-restrained

who are already marked
into zones by straps begin to divide,

loins sinking toward buttocks,
cleft toward cleft until
the first tear is made into two humans—
the one who wants to die

& the left half that will draw all the organs
into altered gravity.
This Saturday I help the muscular nurse

push chairs,
against the rules go in where she does,
wanting to understand

graffiti that says "don't look for me"
or "God took my children first,"
wanting at last their wanting,
wanting to bring them all back
for whom we sang.

VI

New Poems

About Night

It's a blindness
the barn owl has memorized in order
to see: when the owl doubts

or loathes its
compromise, it goes heavy in the familiar
pine woods, & simple light
(though here on Inverness
ridge light's only mongrel greens & grays

less gray) will not hold the bird up.
It's almost night
by the time the short-pants hikers queue
for the last Point Reyes bus,

chatting Gortex & freeze-dried stews.
Rain off the Pacific's begun to thin
all colors, whipping up
the thrift-store smell of old eucalyptus

trees around the ranger post,
coating equally prey & raptor.
How I love going blind

into this ride,
the bus headlights smearing
into firs & the greedy
laurels that for sun have twisted themselves
ugly between bigger trees,
our windows slowly taking the darkness

of the world outside.
An hour to San Raphael—
I'm over a rear wheel, taking the road,
wading into it with my legs

fighting the cramped seat, waiting for sleep
to smudge everything,
my wings, of course, only metaphor.

If she forgave his loneliness,
the soap my mother
complained her German father-in-law

cooked in the small winter cellar
stank: *willensstark,*
strong-willed, he said, I think of the mix,

but might've meant "passionate,"
his word for her. He said I will be the dog
of your dog as he cursed

nobody but himself, a widower,
his galluses down, under the cellar's one bulb.
The soap he thought he stirred

for us was wood-ash lye & anonymous
animal fats— a pioneer soap
he prayed to in German so circuitous
& glottal that whatever his hurt

should've dissolved in it,
though the soap hardened piss-colored
& so cursed that it bit

sores on whatever hand
caressed it. We read WWII a second time
from the news-wrapped cakes:
a few inches of bombed-out London,

Omaha Beach, or a Wehrmacht boy-soldier
sticking to this or that cake's toxic yellow
so that we seemed to wash away

guilt with only the pain the soap gave.
The hands, he said, explaining away

a few times the solipsism
in his eight-year labor, the hands at least

are brothers, but the brain is alone.

BIRDS

     Such syntax the birds work
out with the worm's name, or varietal berries
they pick up
in surprise because hunger's

only the osmotic
clotting between the bird & the thing
in an exchange of cells,
& each chirp that seems so private
begins as neural ghost

the thing eaten first speaks,
the way my father spoke
two years to cancer as it fluttered

around his kidneys,
pecking & pecking in reply until glut
became a kind of cure
from which he died, expecting wings

to lift away the pain.
Which of us is worthy even of the sparrow?
My mother forgave birds

because she couldn't admit them
as metaphor, though she wasn't in our yard
when the jay screamed

the only meaning it had
to our son's goldfish but not to my wife
who, hearing the phone scream

& not the jay, going for that call
& not the goldfish
in its bowl she'd left outside to wash,

agreed to the jay's hunger— deft
& delighted to maim,
how the jay must've hopped in slow self-arousal!

EEYORE

Because I am my family's reader,
I'm sounding out
      Eeyore's lament;
Grandfather in the rest-home bed
      delighting

in his donkeyishness twists
      to move sun-dots
off his face, grumbling German.
I'm seven & Winnie-the-Pooh's afraid—
      under my finger

he's eaten all the honey.
I read further: Eeyore will have no birthday
      gift but the licked-out pot!
Is there a German word back to the honey?
      The nun who'll help him

with his shot twitches one window shade
      to move the sun
in dots down to Grandfather's broken hip

then rattles the needle-tray & insulin.
      This day I stay,
the book closed on Pooh's cupidity,
      to see the needle part
of the ceremony in which Eeyore hurts himself
      for his inability

to process sweetness.
I'll smell the animal smell in the room
      when he touches himself with the needle
& the old man's-smells
      in the thrice-changed

sheets earlier men have died in.
    Poor Eeyore sewn
so many times & the self
    still leaks out.
The syringe feathers into its puncture—

    I look away when I see red,
& I won't read further no matter
    how the nun coaxes.

ANNA KARENINA

Garbo's 1935 "Anna" shows
her in chrysalis preparing to open
    her bloodied wings
against the train wheel a shivering trainman
has tapped & tapped again

for soundness.
Levin taps at her portrait
    in her late Part 7 epiphany;
he may think of oleographs

    of the saints
before whom those sicker still of placebos
cure. Tolstoy, who was Anna
    & Levin both, kept them two &
virtuoso in their different

cries— what gestures you & I took
reading it all that first Chicago
    winter of our marriage,
wind in the plastic I'd nailed
over all windows,

such cold, & snow
the irregular nub-grain in linen.
Our dilettante poverty, our stock soups
    & bakery seconds—
metaphors. Marriage, like Schnabel
    says of playing Mozart"...too easy

for children, too difficult
for adults."
    Forgive that betrayal,
my adult sneer which was to tell
you Tolstoy died

mean & Jesus-ridden,
    at 80 denying *his* wife,
fleeing her in winter, 3 days by foot
&, like Anna, by train:
    I was a new husband,
poised to fail

you & you an anarchy of desires.

BALL

The owner of the softball refuses
street-war rules,
so only some cripples & one woman bat

irresolute, baited by the camp's Viet
vets & freight train vets
who say the game's not real.
The transient camp's only one spigot

in a mown few acres,
ragwort in the margins & Calif oaks
dusted high in the upper, blistered leaves.
Tents & galvanized lean-tos—
everything is the same khaki

or gold resin sweated out of the peeled
saplings & sumac prongs
on which these men hook the excess

by which they're capitalists:
grommeted GI rain capes,
a shared towel rubbed into mere friction
& crusted holes, a cap, that ball.
But the ball's not an argument

against injustice,
even though the church's blue pick-up,
re-crossing the boundary
river to them, runs
over it, not an analogue

for the godly metabolizing the poor
out of their own need
to give from the truck's 30-gal stew vats,
the metal wet with coagulant spill,

rattling as the truck wheel passes over

the missed ball, squashed ovoid
now, its seams yielding.
Either none of this happens according to rule,
or all of it.

RAFTING

How many hours long
the six of us water-
wet, sitting in wet, wet too

fishy-slick with one another's sweat—
not erotic, wanting
only the vague group-self
Ted first refuses then says gloom too

metastasizes, & grins. Thin
& all angles
like coathangers fighting
under his thin
flannel shirt, he pulls two-handed

at the knitted cap to show
by inches he's lost
all hair to chemotherapy— it's the head

he says that makes it hard to die
& in his logic
gives the cap, sinking, to this stream

that is all argument & white
haloed rocks.
Two couples, Job's comforters,
& his wife bumping kapok
swim vests, we're giddied
by sun & all day a dramamine-fed

euphoria: low birds
& river-stone uvulae with the river's song
louder in them—
the whole raft fabric thrums with it,
cling-ropes staccato,

the noise unraveling then miles more

to gravel beds that barely scratch
the river into ripples.
Ted, up wobbly at our shoulders, salutes
the sudden high banks,
the bird-spattered blackberry

canes, a few duckweed stitches
holding this brief earth
& then we slide midstream
again into luster,
bewildered because the sun repeats

oranges in our hands Ted urges
us to eat, apologizing
for the concept *thirst*
at the same time he praises sun.
Ted's wife chokes

at the orange in her hand flaring
out of cloudy white pulp;
it bleeds through her fingers,
but she chokes down
all of it, thirsty for her own choking
not for the orange.

ITALY: CARRARA #8

for Roger Vail

You want us to look until our eyes
carry us out this dark
80 ft high hole beyond our friend Oliver

Jackson the painter, diminuated but blurred
into something still human
by the camera's need to slow light.

This photo's about marble so white
& dense that the eyes
catch fire with the friction

of looking until they burn out against
the quarry wall opposite
where light curdles to palest marble.

The waste rock scabbed off the sides
& sort of ceiling above us
is a mistake light made before marble

shone— the white it takes
200 million years to repel all color.
The other seven photos brought us this far:

past a test slope bulldozers scrape
creamy as a tooth— to look at machinery
I think is from a marble sawmill;

it's bulky in a hairdo of toothed cables.
The afterlight of such labor
coats everything— even the river

Carrione that twitches
powdered marble like fleabane
from its dirty back.

What I learn to see is the black & white
gnostic terms by which a camera sees
each object has integral light,

each thing its own dawn
the eye wants to absorb as much as the camera
does, admitting light

is what things are, & darkness
is only the eye's physiological weakness.

THE LADDER: ROGER VAIL'S PHOTO OF A
ROCKFACE IN THE CARRARA (ITALY)
MARBLE QUARRIES

Imagine a world so heavy
that even the sun is squeezed dark!
As this photo imagines the world,
all light is pinched
out onto three toothed cables that saw the world

horizontal. Only the photo's tiny
ladder (lower right), so small
that maybe it's only the genetic imprint
of a ladder is the way

up out of the blackness.
Imagine what it takes to make this world,
imagine so much of everything—
tractors, BIC pens, Spandexed teen flesh—
so much of everything that it crushes

itself homogeneous & to go on being human
means to want pain,
to suffer so many sawcuts for the sake

of beauty! Forty-two years ago,
when the two county cops
dragged an Iowa limestone quarry
pool for Billy Thiel's body,
I watched the sun
on the wet trawling cable saw up through
the blackness all that muggy Labor Day,
the cop boat dividing the world

into boat-width strips.
Swim? God, no, I'd never swim there,
but every day afterward I put
a toe down, dropped a coin,

my sister's doll's arm, something human,

until all of me was in the blackness.
Now I know I'm balanced on a ladder of humans,
blackness to my chin.
I can only intuit all of those under me,

sway as they sway—
there must be a man under the man
whose shoulders I'm standing on.
Over the blackness, two cops, inquisitors, row.
The fat one (I see only his outline)

bends out of the john-boat to me—
"do you abjure," he whispers,
"do you abjure?"

ROGER VAIL'S PHOTO OF A WORKED-OUT MOUNTAIN IN THE CARRARA (ITALY) MARBLE QUARRIES

This is the mountain before which
art is helpless
& only self-recrimination—
the metaphor is marble

a mile thick under the Apennines.
Orphaned out of corroborating poor rock,
marble the color of linen dried

at the armpit, & so many other whites
nacreous or wild
with amethyst accents (a kind of marble

neurosis). Maybe art helped
Michelangelo's muscular
Slaves to half-climb out of marble

by themselves, but pietàs will crack
with human feelings.
An art that makes gods human

curses humans—
how many weak gods died out
in marble, all Argus
eyes or genitalia & the one god

left over is soliloquist
to Dante whom local quarry legend puts
here above his hell

inventing verbs for the sinned-on flesh,
while, ironically, 700 years
elsewhere on this same mountain,
a quarry workman in corduroys
& cheap Zagreb workshoes cuts out

a new god so hard
that the man goes deaf at the marble
saw whining acerbic disbelief.

CHICAGO PLASTICS, 1960

That whole June of nightshifts,
the only one in a quarter-acre
    of other machines,
my machine made dolls—
how the foreman cursed each re-tooling

for heads or the dozen legs
then half-legs where the sheets dwindled
    like cheap waffles,
the saps & unset flesh
    hardening to scrap.
All night the inexact
setting dies ran flesh-colored

plastic hot on my stuck shoes—
at 2 AM coffee-break, I once drew toes
    on my plastic-coated
shoe tops to amuse the epileptic

    sweep-up man.
One night I'd scratch fingers
where the toes should be;
    the next night he'd ask
for a toothed smile

on the shoe's leather
before the tepid plastic refused
    my lyric little truth.
Smells & subliminal itch—
the hair on arms was burnt
    woolly, my eyes watered:
I seemed bent

    congenitally to the machine
so that I could lip-read the ooze.

By 4 AM, the machine opened
    & closed so quickly
on the liquid that my atrophied hand
    could hardly seize one Clara

before another Clara pulsed over her.
    "Beautiful doll," I sang
in a falsetto, endlessly extruded whisper.
But my song wasn't for women,

or lamenting the smug war dolls:
lack of sleep taught me
    to stare faces
onto what the machine ruined—
the double order of male parts
    we ran late, the women
with little breasts like bee-stings.
I cursed & breathed back

    into the machine
the toxic residue of those parts
on which sex is not yet printed
    even after the dies shudder

over them, human larvae
with diminuated wing-joints, little knobs
    where they attached
to the plastic molding sheets.
    My own shoulders ached

from the effort of being aloft;
    my spit seared zeroes
on the metal in front of me.
    "Beautiful doll," I sang
until a July night I couldn't keep rhythm

to the machine's castanet-
      clicks as it spit
successively scabbier plastic bodies,
on the conveyer the jammed-
      up packing boxes snapping
seams, compacting
      into layers of box-flesh

that shredded against the conveyer's pylons
      until a faraway circuit blew,
releasing the machine
      & me from our dance.
Then my sleep could bleed into me,

make my legs twitch like a long-distance swimmer's.
      My body went soft;
as the foreman let me out into Chicago,
      he had to hold me,
he had to articulate my limbs
to his as he walked me.

—

ABOUT THE AUTHOR

Dennis Schmitz grew up in Iowa by the Mississippi
River and was educated at Loras College and the
University of Chicago. Since 1966 he has taught at
California State University in Sacramento. Among
the recognitions his poetry has received are three
NEA fellowships, a Guggenheim fellowship, and the
Shelley Memorial Award from the Poetry Society
of America.

COLOPHON

The poems in this book were typeset in 12 point
Centaur, originally designed in 1914 by Bruce Rogers.
The book was printed on 55 lb. Glatfelter (an acid
free paper) by McNaughton & Gunn in Saline,
Michigan. Text and cover design by Carrie Andrews.